MIND HACKING

---

*BRAIN HACKING TECHNIQUES
FOR GROWTH, CHANGE YOUR
MINDSET BY REPROGRAMMING
YOUR SUBCONSCIOUS*

Table of Contents

Introduction

Success is a relative term, but something all of us strive to achieve in different capacities. Some of us strive to become financially stable and independent so we can stop living from one paycheck to another and do everything we really want without worrying about the next utility bill to pay, while others are focused on living each moment to its fullest and try to seek happiness in whatever they do.

Unfortunately, many of us forget about the one tool all of us possess, but not all of us actually utilize to achieve the success we are so desperate to accomplish- our mind. It is a beautiful and an incredibly powerful tool whose power, if we realize and harness, can help us materialize anything we ever want. This is backed by science and is not just a theory, but reality. If we only tap into the power of our subconscious mind and harness even some of it, we can be an incredibly powerful version of ourselves and can do things we would have never dreamt of.

For most of us, the subconscious mind is a mystery because it is not something physical we can touch or comprehend fully. Yet science tells us our thoughts, feelings, impulses and life decisions such as who we marry or the career path we choose, are all influenced by our subconscious mind. Isn't it puzzling how we have so little awareness and control of our subconscious mind, yet it impacts our entire life?

Most of us let our subconscious mind go on autopilot. Sometimes, it leads us to make the "right decisions" regarding our life aspirations, career path, or partner. While other times it seems to sabotage us with addictions, attraction to the wrong type of relationships, poor money habits, or repressed negative emotions. If our subconscious mind is so powerful, what will happen if we program it to work with us instead of against us?

In this book, we will get to understand more about our subconscious mind and learn practical ways to positively transform to help us achieve success in our lives.

Your subconscious mind can be your greatest ally or greatest foe. Whether it hinders or helps you live a great life is entirely up to how you program it and above that, how you use it to propel yourself away from things you do not want and towards those that you want.

At the most basic level, your subconscious mind is in charge of your automatic thoughts and behaviors. Since a large percentage of your life is a reflection of your habits and most common thoughts, when you exercise control over your subconscious mind, it becomes easier to ensure that your habits and thoughts are good and therefore, you are living a life that aligns with your highest desires.

To live a great life, a life where you are not only enthusiastic but also capable of making the habitual changes that drive you towards progress, prosperity, abundance, and whatever else you desire in your life, you need to learn how to control, reprogram, and make your subconscious mind work for you. This book is going to show you how to do that.

Are you interested in learning more about that? Well, if you do, this book is a detailed guide on the power of the subconscious mind and will guide you on how to tame, reprogram and control your subconscious mind to do exactly as desired.

Let's get started then and begin the journey to a new, happier you.

Chapter 1: What is The Subconscious Mind?

The different experiences that you encounter in life are not always sudden and because of your good or back luck, however you choose to define it. Those experiences are a manifestation of your thoughts and feelings, and no matter how much you deny it, your subconscious mind does have quite a role to play in that. Intrigued?

Your intrigue here is legit, but it also shows how oblivious you are to your own power; a power locked inside you waiting for you to tap into it. A power so strong that it can beautifully transform your life, and a power that has been given to you so you live an empowered life.

This power is possessed by your subconscious mind and while many people believe it to be something you cannot unleash, it is quite a doable task and just requires you to comprehend how your mind functions.

Understanding How the Subconscious Mind Works

In your mental realm, it is responsible for making sure you stay in your comfort zones. It keeps you thinking and acting the same way, consistent with what you have said and done in the past.

Have you experienced fear or discomfort while trying to do something that you have not done before? You could be trying to speak up in a meeting and right before you open your mouth; somehow you freeze, afraid and uncomfortable?

The subconscious mind is that stifled voice inside. The one that whispers and tells you that it's impossible to balance on two wheels the first time you try to ride a bicycle. It will keep at it, discouraging your attempts, reminding you of every reason why you can't. You may as well stop trying and feel that good feeling of being back to your familiar place.

Every thought that you allow to dominate your mind, creates your reality, thanks to John here who is always watching, listening and recording. Regardless of what you say you want or the things you promise yourself to achieve, if there is no data to back up the fact that this is possible, you will always fail and find yourself stuck in a rut. This must be the reason why habit change is so damn hard.

Now how you choose to perceive your reality will determine your experience in this cold world we live in and believe me it could be fucked up as hell. But it all lies in your mind. Whatever you frequently plant in your subconscious mind, it nourishes that seed and grows it into a plant. That said, oftentimes we engage in this activity quite unconsciously. We may not even be aware of what we are thinking or how that one simple thought is affecting our personality, behavior and life.

Similarly, we may not be aware of the many practices and activities we are actively engaged in that are not affecting us very positively. To pull yourself out of certain activities or encourage yourself to become engaged in other activities, you first need to be aware of what you are doing wrong and what you need to do in its place.

You need to realize your mistakes and shortfalls so you can then actively work on them in the right way, and you must be aware of the improvements you wish to bring in your life so you can then plan accordingly for them.

To move towards better things in life, you need to first inculcate the awareness you need to understand what is wrong and what you want.

Become Aware of Your Deepest and Genuine Desires

To shape your life, the way you want it to be, first understand what is it you want from your life. Quite often, we chase things we only think we want, but don't aspire for genuinely. You may think you want a BMW, but in actuality, you may still be happy with your old Honda and really yearn for inner peace.

To make your subconscious draw the right things towards you, you need to be first clear on your wants and ambitions yourself. Unless you have the clarity of what you want, you will never get the desired outcomes. You may be getting things close to what you want, but you will never be truly satisfied because you don't receive what you want. You may keep blaming your fate for that, but the truth is you don't have complete clarity of your goals. To make your subconscious mind focus completely on your goals, first figure them out yourself.

Sit somewhere peaceful, probably somewhere, you feel relaxed and can think deeply and ponder on your heart's deepest and most genuine desires. Think of the life you wish to live and how you wish to be as a person. Take one thing at a time and get clarity on that.

Start with an area that you are most concerned about, which is mostly finance for most people. Think of how much money you would like to earn and what things you think you need to change for that outcome.

Write down in detail everything you feel is not right in your life and all the things you wish to replace the undesirable things, situations and experiences with. From your addictions to bad habits to the constant stress, you experience to your inability to socialize with people to your constant surrendering to procrastination and to everything else, you are not pleased with.

Also, write down how you wish to improve on these things and go through the lists a few times to ensure you have jotted down everything you genuinely want.

The Benefits of Controlling Your Subconscious Mind

The most amazing thing about your subconscious mind is that it never gets tired, which is why it works all the time even when you are sleeping and always obeys orders relayed by the conscious mind.

While the subconscious mind does indeed control a large swath of your processing power and your life, it cannot do so without direction from your conscious mind, which is why the subconscious and unconscious mind only delivers the feelings, emotions, habits, and behavior of that which takes up the most space in your conscious awareness.

Better Relationships

Of the many mental tasks handled by your subconscious mind, one is the ability to connect memories in your unconscious to present stimuli presently in your conscious awareness.

Working together, the three minds combine old memories to new one thus helping you determine how to manage specific relationships by determining things such as what to say when. When your mind can easily relate what you or someone else is feeling to something you have experienced before, it becomes easier to create a trusting connection. This alone has the ability to improve all your relationships.

Untapped Power

This translates into a well of untapped power that when you decide to tap, will change everything about your life including how you think and reason, how you (or your ability to) achieve your goals, how you relate with others, your level of satisfaction with your life, your success and happiness, and everything else touching every pillar of your life.

By reprogramming your mind, you can change any aspect of your personality. If you want to be more loving and less angry, visualizing yourself as a loving, less angry person and then using affirmative words to reinforce this state will make you a more loving and less angry person.

Likewise, if you want to adopt healthy habits one at a time, by consciously focusing on the habit you want to adopt, the conscious mind will transmit this information to the subconscious mind, which will then determine its importance and ask the unconscious mind to bring forth the memories attached to this.

Another aspect of subconscious mind is that we also call it the universal mind because of its innate connection with the universe. The programs most run by your subconscious mind influence your thoughts and behavioral patterns. When the programs are positive, your thoughts and emotions will be positive meaning, thanks to the law of attraction, you will attract into your life similar emotions and experiences.

How to harness the power of the sub-consciousness?

The first step to harnessing the power of the sub-consciousness is to tap into its vast intelligence, wisdom and knowledge. Before any programming has to be done on it, you must first learn how to reach into the sub-conscious part of your mind naturally and with as little effort as possible. Of course, the first few times that you tap into your sub-conscious would not come easy. But once you master the tricks, you can move on to programming and harnessing its unbelievable powers.

Create a vision of where you want to be what you wish to achieve

Want to get the most coveted executive position at work? Think about being promoted and enjoying the perks of getting that particular job. Vision, in the context of the sub-conscious, however, is not something you just visualize and think about. It has to be a vision that gets you so excited and motivated you will do anything to get what you want without necessarily stepping on someone else's toes. This is because dreaming of something in epic proportions will encourage you to pursue your own goals, regardless of what obstacles that will come your way. Even if you find yourself overwhelmed with too many things too quickly, you will be able to refocus and keep your vision alive.

Include meditation in your daily routine

Meditation is one of the many ways to create a link between the sub-conscious and conscious parts of your mind. It helps you reach a state of conscious sleeping, where you will have the energy or creative ability to tap into the power of your sub-conscious. Remember that you need to take it easy when dealing or tapping into your sub-consciousness, so a state of relaxation and stillness, with your mind clear of any obstructions, will help you reach that part of the iceberg that is not readily accessible.

Visualize as frequently as possible

Think about how easy it is to complete the one project that serves as a determining factor in your promotion, and that one moment where the position is awarded to you. Envision the applause as your name is called and the many congratulations that will follow afterwards. But don't just visualize once a week or every other day. Do it daily and you will be empowered to do, act, feel and dress the part, in preparation for that promotion.

Listen to that little voice inside of you; your instinct

Your subconscious mind speaks through your instincts. Sometimes you may be facing a challenge or having a dilemma and some thought clicks in your mind in a split second, and you have this feeling that it's the right decision. When you learn to listen to this voice, you learn to connect with your subconscious mind and communicate with him.

Engage and tap into your creativity

This is why you will find that people express themselves through art, music, poetry or any creation that makes them feel like they have 'vented' what they feel deep inside. For this reason, whenever you feel like say singing or writing an emotional song, just go for it. Don't go and think that's its dumb to write your emotions on paper. Helping yourself is more important than that little pride of yours. Plus, nobody cares whether you write them, sing or howl them.

When you feel like drawing, draw. What matters is what you want. This helps you come alive and to live more authentically and in close contact with the subconscious mind.

Believe that it is possible to reach your goals

Any form of doubt, hesitation, and negativity will stop you from turning your dreams into reality. Think about how easily you will be discouraged if you spend even just a second to think about the "what ifs" and the bad things if you do this or that.

Always stick to positive thinking and self-talk

Subconscious mind is incapable of questioning whatever doubts and disbelief that your conscience mind has. This is why you need to foster positive thinking, and happy and harmonious thoughts. In doing so, your sub-consciousness will only nurture positives. In the event that you find it hard to stay positive all the time, develop the habit of positive self-talk. Self-talk is a process where you question, analyze and generally muse on the constant flow of thoughts that go through your mind. If you maintain a positive outlook on anything and everything you think about, your sub-conscious will only have notions that are beneficial, useful and positive.

Avoid limitations or distractions

It is important that you do not set time limits as to when you will reach your goal. Accept that things will happen in their own time, and it will happen no matter what. So, if you always have time frames in all that you do, use your consciousness to remove them.

It would also help if you avoid absorbing anything unnecessary, such as idle chatter from people around you. Focus on what you want and eliminate anything that you don't want or need.

Be attuned with your inner self

Intuitive thoughts are self-sending messages from your sub-conscious, directed to your consciousness. Listen to them and act on them when and where it is appropriate. You can take up a hobby that interests you and brings out the creative side of you, to help you learn more about your inner self.

Use sleep to tap into the positive memories of your mind

Rather than go to sleep worrying and thinking about everything that is wrong in your life, relive a good memory and think about it repeatedly until you fall asleep. This allows you to connect with your sub-conscious and instantly creates a good feeling.

How to ask your subconscious?

Whether you are awake or asleep, your subconscious mind is always working. But the best time to ask your subconscious mind is when your conscious mind is not working actively e.g., sleeping, walking, lazing at the beach.

Muscle testing

There is a pure energy that runs through the muscles in our body. We can use muscle testing as a form of biofeedback to help us get answers from our subconscious mind. In muscle testing, things that are "no" will weaken our body, while "yes" will strengthen our body.

A simple way to do muscle testing is using a single hand muscle testing technique. Simply touch the tips of your thumb and index fingers together to form a circle. Now try to break this circle using your other hand's index finger. When you are ready ask your question. If the answer is positive you won't be able to break the circle. Likewise, if it is negative, the connection will break.

Sleep on it

Do you notice sometimes when you try very hard to remember something e.g., somebody's name, it won't come to you? Instead it will appear out of nowhere when you are relaxing in bed? In the daytime, your conscious mind is working hard and trying to solve problems. Night is the best time to allow your subconscious to take over.

Subconscious writing

- Find a place where you can write without disturbances

- Write your question down on a piece of paper

- Without any censorship, write down all the words, thoughts, and ideas that pop into your mind regarding your question

- Keep writing even if it doesn't make sense to you

- After you have finished, do not process it yet but wait till the next day

- Review what you have written with an open mind because the solution might not be what you are expecting

- The answers might also come to you when you are doing something unrelated

Trust that whatever questions you have, your subconscious already has the answers and you are just drawing it out. Lastly, remember, for the power of your subconscious to work, you must have faith in it.

How to Make the Subconscious Mind Work for You?

The human mind, especially the subconscious part has great powers than most people have tapped. They chose to live and let life pass them by, letting the mind control them, screwing up their lives – mind you, that mind of yours has the power to screw you up or make you great. What makes the difference? What you feed it; what you plant in the garden – your subconscious.

You can distort your reality by changing the things you plant in your mental garden. This is to mean you have complete control of your mind and you can train it to think different. You can make it think in a way that creates a path for you to become awesome and attract success.

Identify the thoughts that are disturbing you

Don't pretend like you don't know them; those thoughts that are always sabotaging your progress. You want to start a business and then thoughts of how impossible it is, because of competitors, huge amount of capital need, you are not cut out to be a business person blah blah blah…you know them better.

If you tune into your thoughts, you can agree with me that they do not just hang loose with no support. They are backed up by some emotion. For instance, the type of thoughts in our example above, are driven by the emotion of fear. To break the self-defeating, self-sabotaging line of thought, you must cut it from the core; tackle the fucked up emotions.

Understand how your subconscious is controlling your emotion

The subconscious likes to ride on emotions. It is important to know that the little sucker loves to kick in when you are down; for instance, when you are feeling uncertain or scared out of your wits by what your conscious mind can perceive.

If you want to control the subconscious, you have to understand how it is sitting on and controlling your emotions. Of course, it is using the stored data of what you have seen, heard or said and referring to past experiences. You cannot erase the data, what you can do is take away the power to use emotions by detaching your emotions from where they are not needed – the subconscious will have nothing to ride on! Emotions won't do anything for your work and tasks. They need you to work your ass off and to start now! Stop bringing those little suckers into everything you do; they will sabotage you big time!

Learn to practice specific visualization

They tell you to practice positive visualization. That's right; you need to see good things coming to you. But we are adding specific to it. Why? Because waking up and visualizing that your day will go well is so general, your subconscious will not even know what you mean. It does not even provide direction for your thoughts.

Give your thoughts good direction by being specific when doing your positive visualizations.

Visualizing simply means to see into the future; to perceive things that aren't as if they were. This is a very powerful technique for achieving success – and what you want. The power to do this comes from our favorite sucker here; the subconscious. Specific visualization is where you train your mind to think of and foresee situations in more specific detail. It helps you narrow down on what you need to work upon so you can act accordingly. Also, it programs the subconscious to take you in that direction.

Why not try something different.

Try talking to and about yourself positively, using positive affirmations. Say good things are happening or are going to happen. Kick that self doubt to the curb and say positive things. Even if they do not get on their feet, you did not go in there defeated. You went like a champ to win and you did! If they didn't like it, they must be dealing with some shit of theirs – which is none of your concern. The point is, even in the face of uncertainty or failure, never fall in the trap of negativity.

Take action!

If you want to change a belief that you suck at public speaking to you are good at public speaking, see it and tell it to yourself, but don't stop there. Take serious actions to make sure you nail your next speaking engagement. Read books, speak in front of a mirror; do whatever you have to do to become the best. Only then will little John start to take you seriously; only then can you change his beliefs.

Try something new and solve problems

Now we are trying to alter your brain; to switch up on the subconscious. Trying new things and solving problems will activate neuroplasticity and help achieve the switch up. Doing something you have never done before forces the brain to stretch, creating new pathways; the more you practice that new thing or think of a solution to a problem, the more the pathways get stronger. The result; your subconscious connections are even stronger and can handle what you want to bring its way – which is tougher than it is used to.

Without new challenges, your brain stays 'old', with no new pathways and without expanding. If you took all the steps above and never tried to expand your mind, the new beliefs and ideas will have nowhere to sit. It won't be long before they wither. Same old brain will make same old screwed up sucker you have been-it has lacked the stimuli to grow.

Chapter 2: How Does Your Subconscious Affect You?

If the mind were to be represented through an iceberg, the visible part would be the conscious mind, while the rest of it, the huge chunk hidden at the bottom, is the sub-conscious part. Based on this analogy, you can see why the sub-conscious can be your ticket to reaching your goals and dreams. It did sink the Titanic, after all, the ship that represents the obstacles that hold you back from reaching success.

The sub-conscious, in a psychological standpoint, is that part of consciousness that is not in focal awareness. It is wrong to think that it is unaware, only that it needs to be brought into focus. In terms of functionality, it serves as a memory bank where everything that ever happens to you are permanently stored. It can then be used to store and retrieve data, thus giving it power to keep your goals and dreams within reach.

The sub-conscious plays a variety of roles, but it is also responsible for quick recall and access to what you use on a daily basis, such as the following:

Memories

Do you need to remember someone's telephone number? Do you ever wonder how you can drive a car without consciously thinking about the entire process? All the details are stored in your memories, and the sub-conscious will tap into them whenever you need them.

Daily programs you run

These refer to your behavior, beliefs, habits, values and other filters. What the sub-conscious does is process the information and then test the validity of the information with regards to your actual perception.

Sensations and their meanings

The sub-conscious tries to make sense of what your 5 senses are experiencing by tapping into the unconscious part of your mind. As it happens, the sub-conscious has a direct line to the unconscious.

Why does it hold the potential to change your life?

The sub-conscious mind is your brain's autopilot. As the patterns of your thinking and behavior deepen and become habit, you will do them on autopilot. This means that, if you develop good habits that will lead to success, you will perform them without thinking too hard or exerting a lot of effort. But to really harness the power of your sub-conscious, you need to be fully aware of it and the many secrets it holds. For instance, it is incapable of processing negatives of any kind. It does not recognize the word not, so telling yourself that you will not gain weight over and over again will have the opposite effect, because the sub-conscious records it as "I will gain weight". The best solution is to tell yourself that you are healthy, you are happy, or you are beautiful and slim. When such thoughts are ingrained in your mind, you will perform activities that will help you turn those ideas into reality.

The same thing is true with making money. If you are constantly thinking "I am poor", you will be miserable all the time and you will never see any other way to change your circumstances. Didn't they say it's all in the mind? When it comes to the sub-conscious, this phrase has never been truer.

How Things Can Be Different if You Harness the Power of Your Subconscious Mind

Oftentimes in life, things don't go as you want them to. Different external factors keep coming your way and instead of deflecting them, you keep caving in to your temptations. While you wish to respond better to such events, you end up only reacting to them by surrendering to the different distractions.

Then there are traumatic events, which often take a toll on your body and mind, and exhaust you to the core. Sometimes, you get back up sooner than you expected, but other times, you just give in to the pain and let it wash you over.

All such events, temptations, distractions and sad episodes weaken you from within and keep you from making the choices you actually wanted to take. They keep you from realizing and unleashing your power from within.

Fortunately, you can change all of that and reclaim your life by simply reprogramming your subconscious mind to think, feel and behave differently. This takes a lot of courage, strength, patience and persistence, but if you keep trying, you can achieve your goal.

You begin by setting certain targets and consciously making yourself respond to things differently. Therefore, if you feel doubtful of your ability to do something, you keep telling yourself how you can accomplish the target and you remind yourself of your strength and capability. A few tries help you nurture that habit and in a couple of weeks, you start feeling confident about yourself.

You then consciously pull yourself out of the negativity and compel your subconscious mind to create a new program, one that suits your motive and helps you achieve your goals.

By slowly reprogramming your subconscious mind, soon enough you unleash its full power and open your treasure chest that had been lying locked for all this time.

You can then harness the power to do anything you want. From losing weight to sleeping better at night to eating healthy to quitting smoking to becoming optimistic to interacting better with people to becoming an eloquent speaker to fulfilling your goal of becoming a body builder to starting your music school to let go of your fears that hold you back to overcome depression to absolutely anything you have ever wanted to do. Even the sky stops being a limit because you know you can do it and prove it to yourself.

You realize that nothing can hold you back, and the only limitation you ever had in your life was the negativity and fear you had been fixating on all your life. All you needed to do was believe in your power and work on becoming empowered from within because it is precisely that element you need to unleash your subconscious mind's true power. As the below quote states,

The journey to reprogramming your subconscious mind does begin with awareness. Now that you are aware of what your subconscious can do for you, you need to equip yourself with the ability to effectively control and reprogram it. The following chapters equip you with strategies to accomplish that.

The Power of the Subconscious Mind

To succeed in life, do things you aspire to do, manifest all your ambitions and push yourself to do your best, all you need to do is to harness the subconscious mind's power.

While you cannot control all the external factors and events, you encounter, you can definitely control and manage your thoughts and your perception of events and it is this perception that helps you turn even the most unfavorable events to your favor.

Your subconscious as already stated above builds your internal program, which makes you react and respond to different things in different ways. When it picks up from your unconscious mind that you have mostly chickened out of doing things that feel tough for you, it makes you nurture the belief that you cannot overcome your fears.

It is important to point out that your thoughts travel out in the universe and draw towards them other thoughts vibrating on a similar frequency. Everything in the universe is composed of energy and has a certain vibration that it exudes at all times. Things that share a similar vibration are drawn towards one another, which is why the saying goes 'like attracts like.'

Yes, even we human beings exude a certain energy and vibration, which is through our thoughts, emotions and feelings. These feelings and thoughts travel out in the universe and interact with other thoughts and emotions. Those that vibrate at a similar frequency then mingle and are drawn towards each other.

Every thought is accompanied by a host of events, experiences, ideas, concepts and people associated to them. Hence, when a couple of thoughts interact, they bring closer all the other factors and elements associated with them.

When you come across someone at a social situation who is as passionate about plantation and is a staunch environmentalist like you, it is because your thoughts and those of that person met somewhere in the universe and had a ball of their own. They then bring you and the other person together because the two of you share the same energy and vibration.

Similarly, everything that you feel is drawn towards you happens because of the thoughts brewed up by your subconscious. All the good experiences you encounter and all the not so happy ones are also brought closer to you by your thoughts.

If you keep thinking about how bad things will happen to you, eventually you will face them. Remember the time when you kept thinking about how terrible your job interview would go and you did end up making a fool of yourself. Also, recall the time when you were sure that you would get your house mortgage approved and even though your credit history was not too good, you knew you had to get it because you had been saving for your house.

Think of other similar events, when you were and were not so positive on certain outcomes. You will be surprised to learn that your confidence and inhibitions did make you experience outcomes according to your expectations.

All of this happens because of the ramifications of your subconscious mind, and if you do wish to change certain outcomes and experiences for yourself, you only need to reprogram this wonderful creation.

How to Use the Sub-conscious to Succeed?

Now that you know what the sub-conscious is, how it works and how to tap into it, it is time to put all the things you learned to good use. Think about a particular goal that you want to achieve. For illustration purposes, let's say you want to learn how to skydive.

When setting a goal, it is important to keep it rational. A goal to learn how to actually fly like a bird is irrational, but skydiving is the closest you can get to flying and something that you will be able to achieve. Unfortunately, you are afraid of heights and you have seen too many people die during a dive. How do you deal with this fear by harnessing the power of your sub-consciousness?

Know what you want and focus on it

So you want to be able to skydive. Focus on it and
don't expand your thoughts to parasailing or
overcoming claustrophobia. How you deal with your
sub-conscious with regards to skydiving will be
different from working out your fear of enclosed
spaces. The approach may be similar, but the thought
process will be different. The idea is to focus on one
goal at a time.

**Identify the sub-conscious patterns that keep you
from reaching your goal**

What is preventing you from going out of your comfort
zone? Is it the fear of falling, the thought of the
parachute failing to open, or the idea that you might
get tangled with your harness when you are about to
jump? It is vital that you talk to yourself with all
honesty, without excuses or masks, the very reasons
that you harbor doubts and fears. In the event that you
can't seem to find the answer, you can always talk to a
friend or get professional advice from a therapist.

The reason that you need to identify the obstacles or
blocks of your sub-consciousness is for you to be able

to openly communicate with it. If you are able to build a communication system between yourself and your sub-conscious mind, the easier it will be to deal with your fears, anxiety.

Practice sub-conscious shifting methods at bedtime

15 minutes before going to sleep, your body and mind will reach that state of relaxation, where you feel your muscles loosen up, your breathing relaxes, your heartbeat slows down, and you feel calm all over. Think of this 15-minute window as similar to meditation, where your sub-conscious is open to receive messages. Conveying a message, however, can be a bit tricky and may require practice of any of the four communication methods.

Visualize the end result

While in a calm and totally relaxed state of mind and body, think about that goal that you so deeply desire to achieve, which is skydiving. Then, create an image of how your life is going to be when you finally succeed, think about the end result. Pay attention to every element that makes the image real rather than imagined, such as the sound, colors, scent of the open air, or the people around you, congratulating your success and giving you a pat on your back. Or it could be just the pilot of the plane giving you the thumbs up. This refer to a video visualization of the final result.

Afterwards, focus on one memorable image that you want to frame and remember for as long as possible. What you are doing is static visualization. You can then mix both video and static visions, switching your view with one from the other. Repeat this pattern every time you go to sleep for the next 21 days and the entire process will become easier to do.

Use good memories of the past

Think of a past memory that made you feel good and relive the actual experience in your mind. When you succeed, you will be able to establish a connection with your sub-conscious. If any of the negative memories creep in, chuck them out right away. Because allowing them into your sub-conscious will have a damaging effect and you are unlikely to achieve your goal of skydiving without the fears or worries. Focus all your energy on the good memories, and think of one that you can relive over and over again.

Be grateful always

People who accept their fate and feel grateful for what they have or where they are now have better outcomes than those who don't. Think about it; if you wake up every day angry with your lot in life, you will never find ways to make your life better. You will end up blaming other people, and completely overlooking the fact that you are alive, you have a family who support you, and friends who will be there if you need them. If you shut them out, the more miserable you will become.

The idea behind harnessing the power of your sub-conscious mind to reach your goals and dreams is to create new programs in this part of your brain in order to change your personality or fix whatever problems it has. Think of your sub-conscious as the program that makes computer applications run. Every time an action is required, the program is retrieved and made to run. If it is corrupted in any way, the action will not happen. In the same sense, if the programming in your sub-conscious has many negatives instead of positives, your life could be unhappy and full of struggles.

Chapter 3: The Importance of Setting Specific Goals

Make a Goal and Commit Yourself to it

Goals solidify your commitment to change and serve as a reminder to your subconscious. Your subconscious mind believes whatever you tell it with conviction so if you create a goal and commit yourself to it by convicting yourself to it, your subconscious embraces your conviction and makes you focus on it.

If you decide to work on achieving financial freedom, specify how much money you aspire to make and how long will it take you to reach the finish line. There always has to be a deadline attached to your goal so you know when it is due and instead of procrastinating to work on it, get started with it right away.

Similarly, whatever goal you have, identify the things you would be willing to do in exchange for it. Once you have set your goal, commit yourself to it by chanting it aloud. Speak out that goal repeatedly, and while writing it simultaneously to convict your subconscious to it. When you do accomplish this goal, you can set another one picking the next area of your life you wish to improve and then keep working on one positive goal after another.

To accomplish the goal you have just set, create a detailed plan of action to dedicatedly work towards achieving that goal. However, to ensure you do that successfully and effectively, you need to make your subconscious mind believe that you are capable of achieving the goal and can do so successfully.

Make Your Subconscious Mind Embrace Your Goal

Your subconscious mind indeed responds effectively to suggestions, be it positive, negative or neutral. Whatever you tell it with complete conviction, it accepts that. The truth is it is designed in a manner that it cannot distinguish between reality and imagination. It accepts whatever you throw its way with conviction. This is both, favorable and unfavorable for you and depends largely on what suggestions you choose to believe in and repeatedly tell yourself.

This is the reason why you have not been able to achieve your goal of becoming physically healthy and mentally peaceful because you kept suggesting to yourself the wrong things over the years. You kept telling yourself how difficult it is to exercise and follow your fitness regimen and how you cannot let go of your painful past because it keeps haunting you. You fixated on all these things repeatedly, which is why you only achieved unhappy and undesirable outcomes.

If only you had made your subconscious mind embrace the right and positive suggestions and convicted yourself to them, you would have achieved exactly what you wanted. If only you had reminded yourself of your goal and told yourself how you can fight your temptations and become fit, healthy and active, you would have accomplished it. If only you would have chosen to let go of your painful memories and dedicated yourself to only being happy, you would have been happy and peaceful.

So what if you couldn't do that in all this time, you can still achieve it and it is doable. You can fulfill all your goals and live a life you have always desired to live. All you need to do for that is to make your subconscious mind accept your goal and shift its attention towards your desired goal. Once it embraces your positive goal completely, it will only create positive thoughts in that direction and make you act accordingly.

Here are some strategies you can employ to achieve that:

Visualize Yourself Achieving the Goal

Visualization is an incredibly effective technique that employs creative imagery to make your subconscious mind feel that you have achieved a goal you wish to accomplish. When you repeatedly visualize yourself fulfilling a certain goal, you affirm that goal to it and make it feel that it is your reality. Here it is important to mention the RAS in your brain. Reticular activating system is a system in the brain created to prevent information overload.

If you commit all the information you pick up to your long-term memory, your brain would suffer from information overload and become exhausted. Your mental wellbeing and cognition would suffer as a result which would only make it difficult for you to function healthily and successfully. To keep this from happening, the RAS is created so it filters out all the unnecessary information out from your conscious realization and makes you focus on only the important things.

You now need to practice this visualization for at least 15 minutes twice daily to commit your subconscious to it. You will be surprised at how committed you become to your goal within a matter of weeks and before you realize it, you will witness amazing things coming your way that would only take you closer to your goal.

Practice Positive Affirmations

Another practice you can engage in to further strengthen your commitment is to practice positive affirmations daily. Firstly, you need to chant the goal you created earlier 10 times twice daily and write it down at least thrice and then you need to chant positive affirmations based on it. If your goal is to become financially free, say 'I am financially free and strong, and wealth flows easily towards me.'

Remember to create a purely positive goal that must not contain a single negative word in it including 'no', 'not', 'cannot' and 'don't because your subconscious cannot recognize these words and omits them from suggestion, and then rephrases them. If you say, 'I will not smoke cigarettes', your subconscious is likely to change the suggestion to 'I will smoke cigarettes.' To better understand this, think of the last time you were told not to do something and you did precisely what you were asked not to.

To ensure your subconscious focuses on the right goal, set a positive goal only. If you wish to quit alcohol, say, 'I have overcome my alcohol addiction.' Also, keep the suggestion present oriented, which means it should suggest you have achieved your goal. Instead of saying, 'I will be a millionaire', chant 'I am a millionaire.' Present oriented goals make your subconscious focus on the goal right now and increase your commitment, as your subconscious cannot differentiate between reality and imagination. Therefore, when your subconscious feels you have achieved something now, it reinforces your commitment and makes you work harder towards it, and draws positive experiences your way in the present moment.

Practice positive affirmations by speaking them out very loudly, clearly and confidently so every word rings in your ears and you become completely focused on it. Do this regularly and religiously just as you eat a couple of meals or even more every day. Make it a part of your routine and within days, you will be surprised at how positive you feel from within and how motivated you become to bring positive improvements in your life.

Anchor Confidence to Your Subconscious

To stay strong in difficult times and bring your awareness back to your goals every time a bout of self-doubt attacks you, learn to anchor confidence, happiness, peace and positivity to your subconscious.

Anchoring is an extremely useful NLP (neuro-linguistic programming) technique that enables you to imbed positive emotions into your subconscious mind by anchoring them to a physical gesture. Every time you practice that gesture, your subconscious is directed to give you a nice boost of the respective positive emotion so you experience it and behave accordingly.

If you anchor confidence to a finger snap, every time you snap your fingers, you will feel confident from within and be able to fight the self-doubt brimming inside you. This technique rewires your subconscious to behave as desired so you experience desired outcomes and work committed towards your goals.

There will be times during the journey when you will feel scared, doubtful, unconfident, negative and depressed. You cannot control external influences and factors, and every journey is adorned with some obstacles so there will be times when you will doubt your ability to move forward, reconsider the pursuit of your goal and will want to quit.

In all such times, it is important to learn to trust yourself again and direct your subconscious mind towards your goal. Anchoring is a technique that helps you combat those difficult times by helping you feel confident, happy, safe, peaceful and determined with just a simple gesture.

Working Towards Your Goals To Make Your Subconscious Work Harder Towards Their Fulfillment

Accomplishments help your subconscious mind understand that you are capable of doing all that you have been affirming it. When your subconscious sees proof of your abilities, skills, talents and strengths, it embraces your affirmations even better and places all its faith on them. This helps strengthen the new positive program you are trying to create inside you so you can successfully actualize all your goals.

Also, as you achieve different milestones and goals one after another, your self-esteem starts to improve. Your self-esteem refers to how much you value yourself and is based on how you perceive yourself. If you have a positive self-image, your self-esteem is likely to be high as well. Your self-image is dependent on how much you value yourself, which relies on the accomplishments you have to your credit. When you actualize your goals, you feel good about yourself, which slowly increases your self-esteem.

As your self-esteem increases, it boosts your confidence and when you feel self-assured, you find it easier to find the courage to set bigger targets, push yourself harder and set out on journeys you have been meaning to embark on for ages.

Doing things that you wanted and achieving your goals proves that you are capable of doing all that you have been reprogramming your subconscious for which only increases your strength, self-discipline and grit. To achieve that, you need to get started with actively pursuing your goals.

Here's how you can do that:

Break Your Goal into Weekly Incremental Goals

Willpower is what you need to effectively work on your action plan. You need to practice self-control every time you feel giving in to your temptations. You need to stay positive when negativity hits you hard. You need to keep your subconscious focused on your goals so you don't lose sight of them and keep working consistently towards them. You need to remind yourself of what you ought to do and what you must avoid. You need willpower and discipline to do all of this, and for that, you need to go slow and easy on yourself.

Willpower is not built overnight; it takes time, effort and a lot of consistency. More importantly, you need to go very easy on yourself and ensure you don't feel overwhelmed throughout the process.

When you set a goal and start reprogramming your subconscious to achieve it, you will feel overwhelmed. As excited and happy as you will be to bring a monumental change in your life, you will be equally overwhelmed and may feel the urge to quit the pursuit after some days.

Your subconscious needs proof to make you work towards your goals and the proof cannot be produced if you lose your motivation just after a few days of working hard or just thinking positively. This is where 'breaking down your goal into smaller, doable milestones' comes in handy. A big goal is naturally going to exhaust you emotionally and dampen your spirits. Naturally, if you are asked to wash 100 dishes, you will feel swamped even thinking about it. However, if you are asked to wash 10 dishes first and then do 10 more after a short break, you will feel less burdened.

The same applies to goal setting and pursuing your targets. Instead of seeing your goal as one, enormous task, break it down into smaller chunks. You need to have weekly incremental goals instead of a gigantic goal spread over a couple of months to a year.

Define Tasks and Steps

If your weekly target is to land a client for your insurance company that buys insurance worth of $10,000 at least, what tasks do you intend to carry out to achieve that? Are you going to attend more social meet-ups to meet more people? Are you going to resort to social media to look for clients? Are you going to carry out cold calling? You need to clearly define all that you propose to do to achieve your weekly target and then detail out the tasks.

Ensure that you get into the minute details because you need to define what you will do to execute a certain task and how you will carry it out. Details are important because they help you understand the effort that is expected to be invested in a task so you are aware of the process beforehand and do not worry about it on the nick of time. Also, many people have the habit of planning right when a task is due which only wastes time. Planning beforehand saves time and keeps you from overthinking at the last minute.

Assign High Priority Tasks Daily

When assigning your tasks for the day or next day, do assess each task in detail to figure out if it belongs to the 'high priority' or 'low priority' category. You already know what the former encompasses; the latter includes tasks that do not give your productivity the much-needed kick. While there are certain low priority tasks that are important for the routine functioning, if a task does not really impact the fulfillment of your goal, keep it for a time of the day when you don't have anything important to do.

Eat an Ugly Frog Every Day

Another great strategy to make your subconscious mind work effectively towards all your goals especially the purpose of your life is to eat one ugly frog every day. Okay, do not freak out, you do not actually have to do that, but just something similar, not as disgusting though. You have to work on at least one important, difficult task every day particularly in the start of the day.

Oftentimes, we keep difficult tasks for the end and later procrastinate on them completely. This influences your productivity, doesn't help in the fulfillment of your goals and also slowly weakens the new program your subconscious is trying to create. To ensure this doesn't happen to you, do one difficult task every day.

Identify all the important, seemingly difficult tasks associated with your goal and work on one every day of the week. If your goal is to overcome an addiction, the difficult task would likely be to manage your temptations. In this case, think of the different activities you can do to avoid your temptations and achieve your weekly incremental goal.

Take Action Daily

Once you create your plan of action, go through it a few times to ensure you don't miss out on an important point and after reviewing it a couple of times, start working on it.

You need to take action right away, and not miss out on a single opportunity to work. Go through the list and see what can be done right away and just do it. If you cannot tend to any high priority task, but can send an email to a potential client right away, do it.

You need to take meaningful action every single day without procrastinating on any important task so you start achieving extraordinary results. If procrastination hits you hard, anchor positivity and enthusiasm to your subconscious so you become motivated to work on your tasks and get started with them before it gets late.

Review Your Performance

As you start working on your action plan, you need to review your performance on a regular basis. When you start with a task, write down its name, details, starting time, ending time, problems you encountered in it, achievements you unlock, any strengths or weaknesses identified and how you pushed yourself to move from the start to the finish line.

Go through this analysis at the end of the day so you can assess your performance in every task throughout the day. On reviewing your performance, think of ways to overcome the problems you have identified and then implement the strategies.

Similarly, whatever problem areas you identify, work on managing them successfully so you can move further towards your destination.

Make Improvements to Your Plan Accordingly

Your action plan is the secret sauce to your success, but do not be too rigid about it. While you need to work on it strictly, you also need to adopt a flexible attitude towards it. When you review it and figure out problem areas in it, make improvements to it accordingly. Revisit your action plan frequently and keep adding positive changes to it to make it as effective as possible.

The journey to your goal will not start on its own. You will have to take that step yourself by working on the guidelines discussed above. During this journey, you will encounter obstacles particularly the tricks played by your mind. Fortunately, that too can be surpassed and we have just the right tricks for you to achieve it.

Staying Focused, Positive And Motivated Towards Your Goals

Your subconscious is indeed the force that can guide you towards the right direction provided you choose the right direction and stay committed to it. Your end goal can sometimes become fuzzy when you keep encountering obstacles and experience setbacks one after another.

Chapter 4: How to Change Your Subconscious?

Visualization

If you want to reshape the reality of your life, start by visualizing how you want your ideal life to be. Our subconscious mind's main language is emotions and images. Write a script of your ideal life and then play it like a movie in your imagination. The more detailed, vivid, and emotional you make it, the more your subconscious will think it is real because it cannot tell the difference. Remember the subconscious is your captive audience. You can transfer your ideas from your conscious imagination to your subconscious to make success happen for you. Do your visualization for 10 to 15 minutes daily?

If you visualize yourself being successful, being stinking rich it is very possible you will be stuck right where you are visualizing that for the rest of your damned life. You don't even know the name of the damn island! And first what is success to you, how are you going to get stinking rich? You don't know? Keep on dreaming dreamer, you are going to be stuck there a long minute. Remember, there is a very thin line between day dreaming and fantasies and visualization.

To use affirmations and visualization to control your subconscious mind and make it do what you want, lace your affirmations with feeling and emotion (we talked about this) and then create a very vivid image of what you want to achieve.

You want success and a good, comfortable life. Here is an example of how you can visualize that;

Define what success is to you and what you want to do with your life? Is it getting a screen play you have been scribbling approved for production or getting your PhD in medicine? Visualize time, locations and actually feel the taste of champagne at the premier party or graduation. This is what I mean by being specific to the core. Visualizing your screen play being produced by that top company will start to give you some direction and mojo for taking the steps needed to get there. Also, you will notice that you will start to pay attention to and be attracted to things, people and opportunities that can help manifest your vision. (Just the same way you would really want to drive a BMW and all of a sudden you start noticing them everywhere – it's not that they have suddenly popped out of somewhere, it's just your subconscious directing you to pay attention to what you want. Those cars were there before.

Write down your specific visions and revise them every day when you get out of bed. It will ingrain them in the part of your mind with a very good memory – the subconscious. You can count on it to remind you what you ought to be when you start engaging in unhelpful and unsuccessful shit. Now it will not just do that. John (remember?) is not that nice – that spineless moron may try to sabotage you. Thank goodness he takes what is given to him; you can train him how to stick to your specific visualizations which will help you create specific goals.

Lucid dreaming

You're aware that you're dreaming. You're in control, and you can influence events. So what? It's not like lucid dreaming is reality, so what's the big deal with being aware that you're dreaming?

For starters, the very fact that you can realize that you're asleep and in a dream state is pretty cool. No longer will you have to wake up and feel like eight hours have slipped by without you having been involved in any of it. Awareness during an unconscious state is both unusual and awesome.

For many people, this is the ideal opportunity to explore different fantasies which otherwise wouldn't be possible in the real world. Sexual fantasies, the ability to fly, or even knowing what it feels like to be an animal are all adventures which are commonly undertaken in dreams. After all, this is a time and a place where you can explore anything you want to, without anyone else ever knowing, and without facing repercussions in the real, waking world.

In addition, lucid dreaming can be very helpful when it comes to overcoming nightmares. Terrifying and haunting dreams plague millions of people; so much of the time they can seem overwhelming and inescapable. However, giving the dreamer back some of the control over the dream can come as a great relief.

This is not to say that lucid dreaming will automatically eliminate all nightmares, but gradually they will become much more manageable. Things don't seem quite so scary if you can see, understand and engage with them more directly.

Another reason why lucid dreaming is so useful is because it can harness this visualization to improve real life. Think of it like a dress rehearsal, or a practice run. By imagining, feeling and experiencing what it's like to live a certain way, it becomes much easier to identify how to achieve that same success in real life.

For all intents and purposes, lucid dreams look exactly the same. However, it's all about awakening that section of your brain that actually notices these subtle details. Notice the fact that the scene is hazy, instead of crystal clear like when you're awake; notice the unusual combination of characters who would never normally congregate together in real life; notice how the steps leading from your front door suddenly become a seemingly endless flight of stairs down the side of a cliff.

If you can pick up on these details while you're in the dream itself, the realization will suddenly hit you out of the blue. The words, 'I'm in the middle of a dream' (or something similar) might actually run through your mind.

That's the point you're looking for. When this happens, you'll know that you're right in the middle of a lucid dream, and that you can control and influence everything you're seeing.

Once you reach that point of being aware that you're in a dream, you can get to work the actual lucid dream itself. That's easy to say, but how do you actually lucid dream?

Most of the time, lucid dreaming feels just like you're able to think clearly (as you do while you're awake), except that it happens while you're asleep. As a result, in order to change something up in your dream, just think it!

These are very simple explanations of how to control your dream, but the basic principle is there. You use your mind to control events in exactly the same way as you control your actions while you're awake.

Inducing a lucid dream

Now that you know what to look for in order to identify a lucid dream, you can turn your attention to actually inducing a lucid dream state yourself.

Lucid dreaming can occur of its own accord – you might fall asleep naturally one day, only to become aware of your dreams halfway through the night.

The first time this happens it will probably be a rather unnerving experience; if you've never had a lucid dream before then the feeling of being able to think while asleep seems totally bizarre and unnatural. However, the disadvantage is that spontaneous lucid dreams are few and far between, so you might be waiting a long time before your next lucid dream fix.

Luckily, inducing a ludic dream is something that you can learn to do yourself. The harder you concentrate and the more you practice, the more successful you'll become. With a bit of luck, after time you'll be able to induce a lucid dream every night – or however often you choose!

In order to increase your chances of success, you will need to create the optimum conditions which are most likely to set you up for a lucid dream. Dreaming itself means that you'll have to be sleeping deeply, so try to get as comfortable and relaxed as possible. Anything that is more likely to make you uncomfortable or interrupt your lucid dream experience should be eliminated.

However, do not assume that lucid dreams will come most easily from long, solid stretches of sleep. In fact, the opposite is true. Your chances of experiencing a lucid dream increase greatly if your sleep is slightly broken.

Think about it: while you're asleep and in a lucid dream, the lines between reality and dreams are blurred.

These dreams are so vivid that they can seem tangible and very lifelike. As a result, placing your consciousness on the cusp between sleeping and waking can help to alter your perceptions of reality.

Hypnosis

Hypnosis is a special process wherein a man or woman allow themselves to be placed in a highly suggestible state of mind. There are several different types of hypnotic inductions, but the main components are deep concentration and focused attention. A person has to be a bit open to hypnotic suggestion for it to work. A person who steadfastly refuses to follow the required inductions out of stubbornness or a desire to call the hypnotist's bluff will most likely not fall under hypnotic suggestions. No person is un-hypnotizable; however, you do have to follow the hypnotic practitioners' instructions to fall into the trance state. Most people have an understanding of hypnotism that comes from television and movies, which is a poor representation of the real process of hypnosis.

When people are hypnotized, they could be said to enter into a hypnotic state. In this state, a person's focus is so deep that they might not notice or be aware of what's going on around them. When people are hypnotized properly, they are highly open to suggestions and other commands. A hypnotized person may feel super relaxed and focused, and they will certainly be much more suggestible.

Most people do not know that hypnotism is a naturally occurring phenomenon. We go in and out of hypnotic states every day, often many times a day. Have you ever been hypnotized by the highway or road to the extent that you arrived at an old address or you weren't able to remember how you somewhere once you got there? You were in a small self-induced hypnotic state. When you zone out in front of the television, computer monitor or smartphone, you literally become entranced.

In fact, during hypnosis, an individual is in a conscious state. He possesses heightened focus and concentration. His imagination is intensified as well. Every other stimulus around him is blotted out. By reducing peripheral awareness, he is able to focus his attention on a specific thought or a memory and his capacity to respond to suggestion is increased.

With this said, real life hypnosis contradicts the popular yet misguided conception of hypnosis in the movies. First off, when a person is hypnotized, he is not in a semi-sleep state. He is actually awake, aware and hyper-attentive, which also brings us to the second point of contradiction. A person who is in a hypnotic trance does not lose his free will. He does not become a slave to the hypnotist.

When a person is in a trance state, he is relaxed. The mind is more uninhibited. The individual is less conscious about his behavior. Notice that whenever you go to the movies you are able to temporarily forget about your problems at work or at home. Whenever people watch a film, they tend to experience feelings of happiness whenever a pleasant scene or a happy ending is revealed. Their hearts beat faster when the monster in a horror flick jumps out of nowhere. This, in itself, is a form of hypnotism.

Our subconscious mind works hand in hand in with our conscious mind. While the latter makes us aware of facts, the former is in the backseat, giving us access to memory. Our conscious mind makes us think critically and realistically and our subconscious makes us think more freely with imagination and impulse.

When we are trying to solve a problem for instance, we assess the facts and brainstorm ideas for solutions consciously, but more often than not, the "aha" moments come to us unconsciously. It's like being stuck on a problem then thinking about a solution out of the blue. The thought comes from our subconscious.

The subconscious is also responsible for the things that we do automatically like breathing. It is also the one that processes and interprets the physical information that we receive through our bodies. In other words, the conscious mind may be at the forefront, but it is our subconscious that works behind the operation. The key to getting access to the subconscious directly without being filtered by the conscious mind is hypnosis.

Keep in mind that the unconscious mind seeks freedom while the conscious mind seeks to filter. What the hypnotist does is to speak directly to the subject's subconscious. With the conscious mind placed in the backseat, the more imaginative and impulsive subconscious is in control. The person's reactions to suggestions and compulsions are more automatic. Because it is the subconscious that controls the body's senses—visual, tactile, auditory, etc.—as well the emotions, the hypnotist is able to trigger the subject's feelings. More than that, it is in the subconscious where a person's memory is stored. Therefore, during hypnosis, the individual is able to access events in the past that have long been buried away. By digging up these memories, psychiatrists are able to help a client resolve his present issues. Furthermore, since the mind is in a suggestible state during hypnosis, it is possible to fabricate false memories. For this reason, psychiatrists must take special care when using hypnosis to access a patient's memory of the past.

Basic Hypnosis

The first step for performing basic hypnosis is to select a comfortable environment. The location need not be completely quiet but it should be free from sudden noises that may interrupt the activity. As you speak to the subject, be sure to do it in a calm and slow manner. Observe pauses with each key statement. In the following script, it is necessary to note that the ellipses mean you should pause after the word. Also, you may choose not to follow the script by word. This only serves as a guide so you may change the words as the situation demands.

- Tell the subject to relax his muscles.

- Ask the subject to rotate his head. Instruct him to gradually remove the tension from the neck, then down to the back, and finally to the legs.

- Next, instruct the subject to focus on his breathing. This helps to slow it down.

- The next step would be to direct the person's attention towards something. The purpose of this is to eliminate any thoughts that might distract him.

- Instruct the subject to close his eyelids. The more you suggest to him that he is feeling tired and heavy, the more his chances of obeying you increases.

- Then, pull the subject deeper into the trance by describing to him how he is relaxing even more.

- Begin the countdown induction by telling the subject that that he is descending towards ten steps.

- At this point, you are to tell the subject to open his eyes but suggest that he is unable to open them. This is done to ensure that he has truly been hypnotized.

- Then, instruct the subject to open his eyes. If he is unable to, then he is in hypnosis. But if he is able to, then it simply means that the person requires a different hypnosis technique. Keep in mind that when done correctly, a state of trance can be achieved by most people in less than a couple of minutes. Another sign that the technique has worked is if you see the subject's eyes flickering or his fingers twitching. Perform a finger lift because this test is difficult to fake.

- Once you are sure that the subject is in a trance, deepen their hypnosis.

- You may now proceed to influencing his thoughts as well as his behavior.

- Finally, you may bring the person out of hypnosis. During the entire process, you are expected to watch the individual's breathing very closely. Each suggestion must be delivered in time with his breathing. You are to speak as the subject exhales and then you wait for him to inhale.

Binaural Beats?

Binaural beats are growing in popularity each year as the research and technology used in this field of study advances.

In a nutshell, binaural beats consist of two sine waves made of slightly different frequencies to form a desired frequency difference. The difference in the two tones is then used to alter the type of brain activity a person experiences. The change to the brain's electrical patterns can then be used to enhance many aspects of a person's physiological and physical state.

Enhancing your daily life practices Many people choose to meditate and exercise. These are two of the great life habits we should all have. Since binaural beats affect each person, differently experiment with these patterns for optimal results. There are many other life habits that binaural beats can help benefit.

How Binaural Beats Entrain the Brain

You will notice that when you take one headphone cup off, the tone becomes flat, when you reapply the headphone cup the tones join together and create the binaural beats. Although referred to as binaural beats, or a binaural beat, the beat is more like vibrating tone.

Each hemisphere of the brain has its own sound-processing center to receive the signal inputs to each ear. Upon processing the perceived frequency, which in this case is 5 HZ, the brain will begin to produce brainwaves at the same rate. This process is known as 'frequency following response'. In other words, the brain is following along and becoming entrained to the frequency state associated with the level of Hertz it is hearing.

As with standard musical compositions, not all binaural beats recordings are created equally. The problem with this is not just a poor listening experience, but also an ineffective recording.

Because of the popularity of binaural beats as a way to manifest the benefits normally associated with meditation, the market has been flooded with poorly created recordings that will have little if any effect on the brain.

The reason for this is that binaural beats can be created using amateur music software. Couple this with the fact that binaural beats fetch a higher price than standard meditation music, and its understandable why so many marketers and chancers have taken to the market to make a fast buck.

The accuracy and subsequent potency of the' frequency response process' is down to the competence of the creator. This is problematic for the user because it is pretty much impossible for someone new to binaural beats meditation to audibly identify "good" recording. Of course, after using the recording a number of times, a person would be able to make a judgment based on the effects they feel. With this in mind, it is important to buy your binaural beats from reputable sources so that you don't waste money.

However, it is possible to judge the quality of a recording on two key factors. And doing so will help you separate the experts from the charlatans.

The first thing to be aware of is download quality. The majority of binaural beats recordings are purchased in mp3 format, which is a means of compressing a sound composition into a small file for the purpose of efficient download and device storage.

The majority of vendors use a sound design comprising ear-pleasing meditation music or simple nature sounds that complement the binaural track. However, the mistake amateur creators make is using any old relaxing music they can find or produce over the track. What they don't realize is that using the wrong sound design can interfere with the frequency response process. Without getting too technical, it is important that any sounds incorporated into a binaural beats recording are subject to professional EQ (equalization),so as not to interfere with the effectiveness of the track. For example: if the sounds added to a track are unintentionally sending beta state frequencies to the brain, but the intention of the recording is for theta state relaxation, the recording is effectively neutralized and ineffective for its purpose.

For this reason, you will find that the majority of binaural beats recordings use simple sounds capes. Many are sparse, featuring little more than light meditation music or a simple meditative accompaniment such as rain or natural ambience. Binaural beats require a soothing, flowing sound design so that the listener is not distracted by abrupt changes in sound or pace. Recordings that do incorporate a slightly more intelligent sound design tend to stick to a hypnotic 16 or 32 bar loop to minimize distraction.

Often recordings are composed using music influenced by Far Eastern culture, particularly in the case of binaural beats designed for meditation and creating a higher spiritual connection.

So it is best to avoid purchasing binaural beats that incorporate drumbeats, heavy percussion and/or intricate instrumentation. The most important aspect of engineering a binaural beats recording is to preserve the frequency response process for maximum effectiveness. For this reason, purists often listen to pure tones without any music overlay at all. However, this can be quite unpleasant to listen to. As long as the sounds cape is professionally produced, there should be no reduction in quality whatsoever.

Meditation

Meditation is the next important step to master, because this will help you to drift into an appropriate state of consciousness. It is also the first step towards visualization, which we'll move onto next.

If you've ever tried it in the past, you'll already know that meditation is an incredibly relaxing experience. If, on the other hand, you're a newbie to the world of meditation, you'll soon wonder how you ever lived without it.

As meditation is so relaxing, you'll need to find a space which is quiet, calm, peaceful and comfortable. Your experience simply won't be the same if your environment is packed with loud noises, plenty of movement, and lots of distractions.

You've probably seen pictures of people sitting cross-legged with their hands placed on their knees, but this kind of meditation works just as well lying down. The choice is yours, as long as you're as relaxed and comfortable as possible.

Practiced for centuries and being vouched by generations, meditation is an incredibly effective practice that reprograms your subconscious, helps create a sense of stillness and tranquility in your mind and helps you to better understand your thoughts, aspirations and desires.

Oftentimes, we become confused about our desires and aspirations, and chase things we only think we want instead of following what we really want. This only creates chaos in our life and takes us away from our actual goals.

Fortunately, meditation offers you an escape from a frantic state of mind and helps you think peacefully on one thought at a time and dig deeper into its root cause. It relaxes your racing mind, helps slow down your thoughts and gives you a break from the frenzy going on inside your head so you can focus on exactly what you want.

If you build the habit of meditating daily, you would find it very easy to think about your ambitions and deepest desires and think exactly on what you want. It makes your subconscious receptive to your goals enabling it to concentrate on exactly what you want.

While there are countless ways to meditate, here is an extremely simple and effective one that works well for beginners.

- Sit comfortably in any pose you like in a quiet spot and close your eyes.

- Slowly and very gently bring your awareness to your breath and start observing it very gently.

- Inhale from your nose and watch your breath as it enters your nostrils, circulates inside your body and then observe it calmly as it leaves through your mouth when you exhale.

- It can be a little hard to observe your breath very calmly and with complete focus particularly because you do not have the habit of doing so. To make the task easier, observe the different rhythmic movements your breath produces in your body. If you observe calmly, you will be surprised to notice many movements that you were otherwise oblivious to. You will observe your tummy rising and falling, tingling sensation in your chest, slight movements in your abdomen and other such movements.

- Keep observing your breath closely for 5 to 10 minutes, or keep the practice restricted to 2 minutes if even 5 minutes is a lot for you.

- During this time, you will wander off in thought multiple times and may even feel agitated because of this. Remember to be calm and patient with yourself in this time and bring back your attention to your thoughts every time you feel distracted. This will go on for a while maybe even a few sessions, but if you consistently keep re-aligning your focus on your breath, you will soon reach the point where you can concentrate on your breath for quite a long time.

- Keep consistent at this practice and do it twice daily. In a few weeks, you will find it very easy to focus on your breath and then one thought at a time. That is the time when you should pick any one thought you would like to dig deeper into to gain more awareness into yourself and your goals. Think about yourself, your personality, things you want to do, your strengths, the purpose of your life and other aspects you feel strongly about, and write down all your findings. You then need to join the different pieces together to figure out your genuine needs, wants and ambitions.

It can take you some time to gain awareness into yourself, but if you spend an hour with your thoughts daily and meditate regularly, you will reach that point.

Subliminal messaging

Brainwashing is the act of being able to convince someone to abandon their beliefs and embrace new principles and values. There are lots of ways this can actually be done, be it good or bad. A good example is when an African is been coerced to embrace the American ethos, ideals, and values once he changes location to America. Conversely, when a new dictator government takes over, they often go through the process of brainwashing the followers to embrace their ways so as to actually convince citizens to peacefully follow.

However, there are different brainwashing processes available but it isn't something that can be easily seen or learned. Predominantly, one major requirement that is associated with brainwashing is 'isolating the person from the public.' The moment the subject is able to be with other people and influencers, they are prone to thinking freely and thus rendering the brainwash ineffective.

Brainwashing is going to be the slow process of taking the ideas that a victim has about their identity and their beliefs and then replacing these with new ideas, ones that are going to suit the purpose of the manipulator. Brainwashing can occur in a narrow and a wide context. For example, a brainwasher could use the techniques in order to control one person, or they could use those techniques in order to control the minds of a larger group all at once.

The starting point of brainwashing is going to be the social circumstances and the mental state of the victim. This is going to be the foundation for the rest of the process, and if the manipulator is not able to figure this part out, then the brainwashing session just won't be successful. Brainwashing is not a process that is going to work out for everyone. It is going to require a good identification of a person who is looking for something or someone who has a void they are trying to fill.

This brings us to an important point. Who is the ideal victim for a brainwasher? People who have had their existing reality shaken up because of some recent events are some great targets for brainwashers. If you have lost someone you are really close to or had another dramatic or traumatic event in your life, then you may be more susceptible to brainwashing.

Once the brainwasher has found their victim, either through the Internet or in person, the process of brainwashing is able to begin. Contrary to the popular image you may have in your mind about a brainwasher, this person is often going to come across as someone who is rational, friendly, and calm. Someone who seems to have their lives together in a way the victim wishes they could have their own. Imagine how it would feel if you were homeless and a celebrity you admired befriended you. This is often how the process of meeting the brainwasher is going to feel for the victim.

The brainwasher is going to get to work right away. The first step for them is to create a level of rapport and trust between them and the victim. This is going to be done with superficial and deep similarities. The superficial similarities could involve some surface level preferences, something like enjoying the same food or sport as the other person.

They will then move on to a deeper level of rapport, some that could involve a deeper shared experience that they had in the past. The brainwasher will most likely fake these, in a convincing manner, in order to create these bonds. So, if the victim shares with the brainwasher that they lost a close relative in the past, then the brainwasher is all of a sudden going to have a story that is similar to share with the victim.

For example, if the brainwasher is trying to convert the victim over to religious terrorism, they would not just start out with the terrorism part. They may initially start focusing on the fact that God loves the victim, something that the victim is likely to accept. The more objectionable ideas, such as God wants you to blow yourself up, are ones that are saved until much later in the process. Once the victim has accepted that last part, then this brainwashing session is at a point of no return.

Affirmations

Affirmations are positive words or phrases that are stated in the present tense to convince your subconscious mind that you have successfully achieved or acquired something when you really have not yet done so. Affirmations help to counter negativity and aid in the visualization of the completion of your goals.

Associating emotional passion with words and images creates a powerful reinforcement of the beliefs and behaviors that are needed to achieve your goals. Repeating affirmations out loud or even silently multiple times each day makes them highly personalized and empowers them to help you to keep your focus on your goal and not on distractions or obstacles.

The trick to saying affirmations that work and can program your subconscious mind is confidence and perceived truth. Simply put, although our subconscious does not know the difference between real or fantasy, our affirmations should not raise internal objections because it is too farfetched. For example, if you are currently broke and unemployed, it might be a stretch for your subconscious to believe the affirmation "I'm going to be a billionaire by this December" as compared to "The ideal job is already mine. My finances are improving every day."

- Write affirmations that have corresponding feelings, focus on the positive, and have no opposing views.

- Face a mirror, take a deep breath and speak your affirmation a few times in the morning, noon, and evening. When saying your affirmation, focus on the meaning and feeling of your words.

- Another method is to write your affirmation several times on a piece of paper daily.

- Repetition and feelings are the key to reinforcing affirmations to your subconscious.

Affirmations also motivate you to take action by reprogramming your patterns of thinking, feeling, and behavior. They must be genuinely felt and expressed to create the intention energy that fuels the manifestation of your goals.

Make personal affirmations. Your mind is not yet that strong to influence external physical realities. Use the first person point of view.

Once you have created an affirmation, state it with passion and conviction (out loud or silently) at least 20 times each day for 3 weeks. Write it on index cards or sticky notes and post them wherever you will easily see them: at home, at work, in your car, as wallpaper on your phone and computer – be inventive.

For an affirmation to successfully help you to manifest what you want, you must truly and deeply believe that you not only deserve your goal, but that is possible for you to achieve it. Without that strong belief and the emotional passion to fuel it and drive it forward, you will not achieve your goal.

You can ramp up the power of affirmations even more, however, by combining them with the power of visualizations. Using them together creates an energy that exceeds what each of them can do individually. Simply visualize achieving your goal and enjoying its results in vivid detail while you repeat your affirmation with as much positive emotion as you can muster.

Example of Affirmations

- I can easily let go of my past and stay focused on the present.

- I choose to be happy.

- I am so happy and grateful that money easily flows to me from all directions continuously.

- I maximize every hour in the day by being productive.

- My home is a clean, warm, and happy place that supports my wellbeing.

- I am beautiful, kind, unique, powerful, and capable.

- I love and believe in me right here and right now, and by definition, I have tremendous wealth, absolute happiness, abundance, and expansive ideas that elevate my life.

- My life has purpose and meaning.

- I am worth it, valuable, and important.

- I have no fear of taking risks and working in different directions, and I celebrate that about myself.

- I am always peaceful and relaxed.

- Today is a new beginning that is filled with many opportunities.

- I am confident, creative, beautiful, blessed, and excited about my future.

- I focus on relationships that are positive, healthy, and make me feel loved and respected.

Make affirmative statements to support your choices/decisions

The thoughts and actions that you put in your schedule every waking day are what trains your subconscious how to be. In case you have entertained dumb thoughts and actions before, you should know that a vision of better will not kick the subconscious to submit immediately and direct you that way.

Repeat affirmative statements to yourself over the course of the day. This gets them ingrained in your subconscious mind. Now, do not just say it, go and take action before the end of the day. Show this damn sucker that you are serious by taking action on what you say you will do. Otherwise, he knows you are not serious and will always screw you over and show you other things that you can do, like sexting with a cute guy who is not your boyfriend, when you are supposed to be reading or doing a meaningful task.

Chapter 5: The Importance of Repetition

With subjective thoughts, repetition is key. The more you enforce positive thoughts, the higher the chances that your subconscious mind will recognize the positive thoughts as important, and the more likely that it shall bend to the will of your positive programing.

At the heart of controlling your subconscious mind is this one thing: the need to change your thought patterns.

Control your subjective thoughts

Thoughts are not equal, which is why our thoughts can be objective and subjective. Objective thoughts are those bred from general reasoning or thinking; a great example here is thoughts bred from study or recollection. Often, such thoughts lack feeling and therefore cannot affect the subconscious mind or get it to release emotions or feelings of any sort.

Subjective thoughts are thoughts existing in the mind and bred from thinking; they are not an "object of thought." When focused on and given enough emotional power, such thoughts have the ability to enter into and influence the subconscious mind. Worry is a great example of a subjective thought. The more you worry, the more anxious and worrisome you will get because the subconscious mind will be communicating with the unconscious and asking it to recall all the times you have worried and implement the habits/patterns you used to handle it.

To use subjective thoughts as a way to control your subconscious mind, use emotion-infused affirmations (positive self-talk). Saying something as simple as, "I am a radiant ray of happiness" and then visualizing yourself as being happy (infusing the affirmation with emotional power), will change the subconscious patterns associated with happiness, the ones in your RAM.

While still on subjective thoughts, you should note that controlling your conscious awareness is a choice, a decision. Make the decision to become aware of your conscious thoughts—especially as you engage in tasks that do not require active brainpower: bathing, brushing your teeth, washing the dishes, cooking etc.—and make the choice to or not admit specific thoughts.

Learning how to observe your conscious thoughts from moment to moment takes tons of practice. The best way to get started on this path is to practice mindfulness meditation.

When you notice negative thoughts, which you will primarily because the mind is negative-inclined—it notices negatives more than it notices positives—do not wish them away. Take a moment to observe the thought, accept its existence, and then let it fade out of your conscious awareness.

To keep negative thoughts from becoming subjective and emotion-laced—meaning they have the ability to affect your subconscious mind—question negative thoughts as they arise and then reword them into positive statements/affirmation.

Use Substitution

Substitution is an effective way to stop negative thoughts in their tracks. As the name of the technique suggests, the idea is to become aware of your moment to moment conscious thoughts so that when you notice a negative thought, you can replace it with a suitable (adjacent and countering) positive thought.

Through the power of substitution, a mind prone to negative thinking can easily become a mind prone to positive thinking. The ability to notice negative in time to substitute them with positive ones takes time to master especially for someone whose mind has grown accustomed to negative thought patterns.

The ways by which you can get your conscious mind to stop concentrating on negativity and start concentrating on the positivity in everything are many. The most effective of these ways, given that making your subconscious mind pliable to your commands happens through the conscious mind, is journaling.

Maintain a gratitude journal (keep it with you at all times) and as you go about your day, constantly be on the lookout for things that fill you with gratitude. Now, assuming you are swimming in negativity, the thought of finding something to be grateful for may seem laughable; it is not.

When you are grateful, you are looking at the things you have instead of the things you do not have; this itself has immense power.

Can you see the difference in thought? Although gratitude journaling sounds simple to a point of seeming ineffective, do not underestimate its power especially when you make it a habit. When you walk down the street looking for things to appreciate in people, the street, passing cars, etc. the effect this will have on your mindset will be tremendous.

Be grateful for everything that adds value to your life. It will teach your subconscious mind to notice the good in everything and because this is part of subconscious reprogramming, the control it will give you over your subconscious will make it your bitch.

In addition, when you get into the habit of gratitude journaling and heaping praise on everything that adds value to your life—or even on random strangers you meet—it will be easier to recognize negative thoughts in time to substitute them with positive ones.

Again, repetition is key. Always remember that nothing worth having comes easy. Practice until noticing negative thoughts and then replacing them with positive ones becomes second nature.

Now that you know how to control your subconscious mind and make it your work for you because you want to achieve success and experience abundance in all areas of your life, you need to learn how to reprogram the subconscious mind.

By reprogram, we mean replace the default programs in its RAM with better ones. For instance, if you are a pessimist/negative thinker, you can reprogram your subconscious mind so that you make positive thinking the default program.

The Laws of the subconscious Mind

For every idea or thought is a physical reaction

The sub-conscious mind operates in the premise that what you think can affect all of your bodily function. That is, if you worry, afraid or angry, you are likely to experience negative physical reactions, such as ulcer, increase in adrenaline in the blood, and accelerated pulse rate. If your idea is associated with a strong emotion, it will definitely reach your sub-conscious. Once the idea is accepted and stored in your sub-conscious mind, you will experience the same exact reaction every time the idea or thought resurfaces.

Imagination is more powerful than reason

Have you ever wondered why some people commit violent crimes based upon what they thought or imagined instead of acquiring the facts first? Well, now you know. A lot of people allow imagination to rule over reason, which explains why they have prejudices, unreasonable beliefs, and superstitions. So if you can control or do something about your imagination you, can turn it into a powerful tool.

Opposing ideas cannot be held simultaneously

A father might believe in true honesty, and even expects his children to be honest all the time, yet still engage in some form of dishonesty on the side. No matter how he justifies his actions, he will suffer the effects of his conflicting ideas on his mind and nervous system.

An accepted idea will stick until it is replaced

The idea that you need a drink to loosen up is not really a correct idea, but the effects of alcohol seem to work because it is a thought that you accepted as true. And, until such time that the idea is replaced with something correct or something else, it will remain in the sub-conscious. Unfortunately, the longer a thought remains, the more opposition it will have for being replaced.

Symptoms induced by emotions can have physical manifestations

If persisted long enough, emotionally induced symptoms can lead to organic change. As what reputable medical men acknowledged, more than 70%

of ailments that affect humans are caused by a malfunction of an organ or other parts of the body that was disturbed by a reaction in the nervous system. What caused the reaction? Yes, something to do with the negative ideas in the sub-conscious. This is not to say, however, that everyone who complains of being sick is neurotic or emotionally ill, just that the mind and body are closely linked that what disturbs one will affect the other. So, if you continue to fear and constantly talk about your tension headache, for example, an organic change will occur in your body and make itself known physically.

A self-suggestion once accepted will have less opposition to other suggestions

Ever wondered why some habits are hard to break? Because an idea has been acted upon repeatedly, it becomes accepted by the sub-conscious mind. And based on the rules of the sub-conscious, the longer it believes on something the harder it will be to alter that belief, thus the difficulty to break the habit. The opposite is also true, however. That is, if you suggest something positive and act upon it, you will be able to move on to more complex suggestions.

For the sub-conscious to respond, the conscious must work less

Experts suggest that, in dealing with the sub-conscious mind, it is best to take it easy. Take for instance when you have insomnia or just having a hard time going to sleep. This is because you are using your conscious mind, exerting a lot of effort to influence your sub-conscious. Unfortunately, this part of the brain doesn't respond easily or quickly when the conscious is working overtime. So, rather than force sleep to happen, allow sleep to happen gradually and without a lot of conscious effort.

How to program Your Subconscious?

Implement the following steps/rules and you will successfully reprogram your subconscious mind:

Clarity of aim

Reprogramming your subconscious mind is a lot like creating goals in that both require clarity of purpose or aim. Before you start the process of reprogramming or make changes to the programs in your RAM (subconscious) decide what you want and then define it as clearly as possible because a lack of clarity is how you attract the wrong circumstances. Remember what we said about visualization: the clearer it is, the stronger the emotional attachment, the more bendable your subconscious mind will be.

Clarity of aim also requires that you load one program the change you want to make—at a time. Reprogramming your mind is very similar to creating new habits—in fact, to reprogram your subconscious mind, habits are the very thing you need to create. For instance, when you form the habit of journaling, using affirmations, meditating, and being mindful, the habits will reprogram and have a clearly visible effect on your physical life.

Know what you want (write the desired outcome on paper), and then if you have several aims, only implement one at a time. Remember repetition is one of the secrets to reprogramming your mind. Focusing on the implementation of more than one aim will only create confusion and discord in your life.

Isolate the faulty 'program'

Whatever circumstance you want to change, you must first realize that your presence in that circumstance comes from a set of programs (habits, beliefs, etc.) you have automatically installed in your subconscious mind.

Before you 'install' a new 'program'—we can also call it habit because repetition leads to the formation of habits—determine the nature of the program you want to uninstall from your subconscious mind. Determine how the program has been keeping you from achieving your goal or the desired outcome. Here, a sincere conversation about why you are where you are right now (the undesired circumstance) will prove very effectual.

The aim of having a heart-to-heart conversation with yourself is to help you determine and isolate the program (the set of habits and beliefs) that is placing blockades on the path to your goal, wish, or desired circumstance.

Asking yourself, "which program, belief, perspective, or obstacle is keeping me from being Y or achieving X?" will unearth the programs you need to reprogram.

By finding the cause, the faulty program, it becomes easier to determine which subjective thoughts, affirmation, and visualization to feed the mind to reprogram habits, beliefs, and programs stored in the subconscious and unconscious mind (the two have a very interrelated relationship).

Do it before drifting off to sleep (or first thing in the morning)

Learning something new—such as a habit or reprogramming your subconscious—activates neuronal connectivity, something that activates our alpha brain waves, the waves most predominant in our mind as we day dream. This resource has additional information on brain waves and their effect on the various levels of the mind:

Reprogramming your mind in the moments before you doze off is the most effective time to do it because at this time, the conscious mind relaxes as the body and muscles loosen, and your breathing rate eases and you enter into relaxation mode, alpha brain waves. In these 15 minutes, the pathways between the conscious and subconscious will be open, and it will be easier to implant thoughts, visualizations, affirmations, etc. that help you reprogram your subconscious mind.

Using these three easy to understand steps/rules, you can reprogram any habit, belief, perspective out of your subconscious mind and replace it with whatever program you want depending on your desired outcome.

Conclusion

Thank you for making it through to the end of this book. The power to do everything that you ever wanted is just inside you, waiting for you to unlock it and trust me, you can do it. This book is right by your side and if you pay heed to the actionable information in it, you will only move in the right direction in life. Anyone wishing to bring about substantial change in his or her life will at one point or the other have to reprogram the subconscious mind.

Your mind makes you; especially that deeper and more quite part which whispers a lot. It's a huge memory bank that basically stores everything that you have lived by and through. It remembers everything and then programs you; defines how you are wired and how you get to live.

This is why when you screw up this part of your mind, your life is screwed as well. Again the subconscious is set to keep you in your patterns and will certainly try to pull you back every time you try something out of your norm.

You can make a change by taming it. This book will help you discover how you can make your subconscious mind work for you and help you create your new awesome life!